To all of the flowers in my life.

The Flower.

*Flowers
Do
Not
Choose
When
&
Where
They
Bloom.
When they do,
It's breaktaking.*

*Every flower has a different purpose
...
What is yours?*

Hello Flower,

You are perfectly imperfect
...
Embrace it.
You were uniquely created
To be
The beautiful you that
You are.

K.

Hello Flower,

Don't allow
Negative energy
To consume your day.
Let your inner light,
Your inner beauty
Shine through
Creating an aura
that attracts the world
To you.

K.

Hello Flower,

Smile.
Just simply, smile.
Because smiles are contagious

...
&
Your smile lights up the room
&
Warms the hearts of those
Around you.

K.

Hello Flower,

A journey of self love
Is the only journey
Worth taking.
Love yourself so much

...

It hurts.

K.

Hello Flower,

Remember,
You
Are
Special
...
No one can be you
No matter
How hard they try.

K.

Hello Flower,

Spread
Positive
Energy
&
Love
Everywhere you go
...
You never know
The impact
You will have
On
Others.

K.

Hello Flower,

Remember
...
If it's for you,
It will
Happen
...
Everything happens
In its
Perfectly, perfect
Time.

K.

Hello Flower,

Surround yourself
With those
Who shine as bright
As you do

...

Weeds must be
plucked
Before flowers can
fully bloom.

K.

Hello Flower,

There will be people
Who try to keep
You from
Reaching your fullest
Potential

...
Smile,
&
Continue working.

K.

Hello Flower,

When you are
Happy,
SHOUT!
…
Share it
with the world.

K.

Hello Flower,

Don't hide
The real
You
...
The world needs
To
Know
Just
How truly
Amazing
You really
Are.

K.

Hello Flower,

Begin
Each
Day
With positivity
&
See
Just how amazing
Your
Day
Turns out.

K.

Hello Flower,

Never
Lose
Sight
Of
You
...
If you lose yourself,
What's left?

K.

Hello Flower,

Be
Your
Own
Cheerleader

...

Cheer as LOUD
As you possibly
can!

K.

Hello Flower,

Stop contemplating about
Starting
&
Just start!
...
Start
Whatever
It is
Your
Heart desires.

K.

Hello Flower,

Think of each
Day as a
"Do-over"
...
Don't like how yesterday
Went?
Inhale. Exhale.
&
Try
Something
New.

K.

Hello Flower,

All
Things
Begin
With you
Believing in yourself.

K.

Hello Flower,

Know
That you
Are
Deserving
Of
the
World.

K.

Hello Flower,

You learn
A
Lot
About yourself
When
You
Venture out
On your
Own
…
Go explore.

K.

Hello Flower,

A pure heart
&
A sound mind
Will help
You
Sleep better
At night.

K.

Hello Flower,

Energies can
Be toxic
...
Be picky with
What
&
Who
You surround yourself
With.

K.

Hello Flower,

Explore the world
to see
just how beautiful
it really is.

K.

Hello Flower,

Try...and fail,
Then try…
&
Fail again
…
Eventually,
You'll succeed
…
What's success
Without failure?

K.

Hello Flower,

Don't be afraid
To
Experience
Something new
…
You just might like it.

K.

Hello Flower,

Live
(adventurously)
Love
(wholeheartedly)
&
Laugh
(until it hurts)
...
It's cleansing to the soul.

K.

Hello Flower,

If you're tired…
Rest
If you're hungry…
Eat
If you're sad…
Cry
…
Live by your own rules.

K.

Hello Flower,

Honesty
Will be
Your
Biggest form
Of
Freedom.

K.

Hello Flower,

Always
Be
True
To
Yourself.

K.

Hello Flower,

Welcome
Change
With
Open
Arms.

K.

Hello Flower,

Voice your
Opinions
...
Change
doesn't
happen
With silent whispers.

K.

Hello Flower,

Free yourself
From
Anything you feel
Is
Hindering
Your growth.

K.

Hello Flower,

Your
Wisdom
Will take you places
You've
Never
Imagined.

K.

Hello Flower,

Support
The
Dreams
&
Aspirations
Of the ones you love
...
Your
Support goes
A
Long way.

K.

Hello Flower,

Protect
Your
Heart
…
Lock it away
&
Only give
Someone
Deserving
Of it
The
Key.

K.

Hello Flower,

Do not
Be afraid
To
Weep
...
The
Tears
You
Shed
Do not indicate
Weakness
But
Strength.

K.

Hello Flower,

Focus
On
The
Quality
Of
Your
Work
Over the quantity
...
Everything you touch
Is
A
Representation
Of
You.

K.

Hello Flower,

Have you ever
Taken
The time to listen
To
The
Stories told
Around
You?
…
You never know
What an
inspiration they
Can be.

K.

Hello Flower,

Some days
Will
Be
Gloomy
...
Don't quit,
You're
Almost
There.

K.

Hello Flower,

Your
Creativity
Should
Have
No
limit.

K.

Hello Flower,

Learn to appreciate
The
Not
So good
Things
In your life
...
They're what make you who you are.

K.

Hello Flower,

You're Beautiful.

K.

Hello Flower,

Sometimes
Saying
Nothing
At all
...
Says so much.

K.

Hello Flower,

At times
you make think
It is
Easier
to wear a fake smile
over a real one

...

Your emotions
Don't need to be
Masked.

K.

Hello Flower,

Nourish
Your
Mind,
Body,
&
Soul.

K.

Hello Flower,

We all
Deserve a
"Me"
Day.
Go out
&
Do
the things
That make your
Heart
Smile.

K.

Hello Flower,

Speak
All of the positive things
You desire
Into
Existence.

K.

Hello Flower,

Fight
Through
Your
Biggest
Challenges.

K.

Hello Flower,

Your
Time
Is
Valuable
...
Don't allow
Anyone
To
Waste
It.

K.

Hello Flower,

Know your worth
&
Don't
Allow
Anyone
To
Diminish it.

K.

Hello Flower,

Remember,
The energy
You
Give off
Is
Contagious.

K.

Hello Flower,

Who cares what "they" think of you?

K.

Hello Flower,

Forgiving
May set you free,
But
Never forgetting
Keeps
You
Wise.

K.

Hello Flower,

Don't be in such a rush
To get through the day
...
Stop to
Smell
The
Sunflowers.

K.

Hello Flower,

Welcome
Love
Into your
Life
&
Allow
Yourself
To be
Loved.

K.

Hello Flower,

Don't
Live
Life
Like
A
Dress
Rehearsal
…
Live each day
Like it's
Opening
Night.

K.

Hello Flower,

Have you given
Yourself
A
Compliment
Today?

...

What are you waiting for?!

K.

Hello Flower,

Love what you see,
When you
Look
In the mirror.

K.

Hello Flower,

It
All
Begins
With
You.

K.

Hello Flower,

Stand
Firmly
Behind
What
You
Believe
In
…
Even if it means
Going against
Popular
Opinion.

K.

Hello Flower,

Don't let anyone
Make you feel
Bad
About the choices
You make.

K.

Hello Flower,

Pay
Homage
To
Your
Roots
...
They
Made
You
Who you are.

K.

Hello Flower,

Fill
The
World
With
Kindness.

K.

Hello Flower,

The battle
With self
Is the
Most difficult
battle
...
A Battle
You should fight to
win
Everytime.

K.

Hello Flower,

Treat yourself to whatever your heart has been desiring.

K.

Hello Flower,

You are strong
…
Don't give anyone
The power
To take your strength
Away.

K.

Hello Flower,

Practice patience
…
It's a virtue.

K.

Hello Flower,

Why judge a book
By
Its
Cover?
…
It just might be
An
Interesting
Read.

K.

Hello Flower,

A new day = A new adventure.

K.

Hello Flower,

Make changes to your life
That
Will
Bring you peace.

K.

Hello Flower,

Step
Out
On
Faith

...

Don't live in fear of
"What ifs".

K.

Hello Flower,

Protect
Your
Energy.

K.

Hello Flower,

You have all the power.

K.

Hello Flower,

Some days will be harder than others
...
Don't
Give
In.

K.

Hello Flower,

Have
Fun
&
Enjoy
This thing called
Life.

K.

Hello Flower,

Remain
Optimistic
...
Even in
Sticky
Situations.

K.

Hello Flower,

Not
Everyone
Is meant
To
Ascend to
New
Levels
With you.

K.

Hello Flower,

Trust
the
Process.

K.

Hello Flower,

Think about your
Number
One
Dream
At the moment
...
Chase it.

K.

Hello Flower,

Define
Your
Happiness.

K.

Hello Flower,

Keep an open
Heart,
Mind,
&
Soul.

K.

Hello Flower,

Cherish
The
Memories
That help you
Remember
The happiest moments in your life.

K.

Hello Flower,

Think big.
Start small.
Work fast.

K.

Hello Flower,

Live
&
Walk
In your purpose.

K.

Hello Flower,

Step
Outside
your
Comfort
Zone

...

Watch
Some amazing things
Happen.

K.

Hello Flower,

Dream
Even
BIGGER
Than you did
Yesterday.

K.

Hello Flower,

Take care
Of
Your
Responsibilities
…
Allowing
Them to linger
Will not make them
Disappear.

K.

Hello Flower,

No matter
Where your dreams take you,
Always
Remain
Humble.

K.

Hello Flower,

Use
Every
Opportunity
Given
To uplift others.

K.

Hello Flower,

Look for the good
In
Every
Person
You
Come into contact with.

K.

Hello Flower,

Open your eyes
...
Sometimes
The
Answer
Is
Right in front of you.

K.

Hello Flower,

Don't
Let
Fear
Cause you to miss out
On
Opportunities.

K.

Hello Flower,

Find
the
Answers
To your own questions

...

You'll end up discovering so much more.

K.

Hello Flower,

Celebrate yourself
&
All of your accomplishments

...
You deserve it!

K.

Hello Flower,

Move in silence
...
Shock the world.

K.

Hello Flower,

Let
Everything
You touch
Turn
To Gold.

K.

Hello Flower,

Excuses are meant
To
Keep
You
From pursuing
Your
Dreams
...
Avoid making them.

K.

Hello Flower,

Cancel out
All of the
"Noise"
That tells you
You can't do something

...

Because you Can.

K.

Hello Flower,

Your
Ego
May try to
Self-sabotage,
In order to keep you
In
Your
Comfort
Zone
...
There is no success
Without
Discomfort.

K.

Hello Flower,

Learn
Your
Likes & dislikes
Your
Weaknesses & strengths
Your
Dreams & fears

...

Learn yourself.

K.

Hello Flower,

Perfection
Does
Not
Exist

...

All that you are doing is more than enough.

K.

Hello Flower,

Genuine
Happiness
Inside
Always shines through
On
The
Outside
...
Glow baby!

K.

Hello Flower,

Give a woman
A
Compliment
Today
...
We need to start uplifting one another.

K.

Hello Flower,

Get up.
Get moving.
Conquer today with lots of productivity.

K.

Hello Flower,

You
Have
Your
Own
Individual path to follow.

K.

Hello Flower,

Listen
To
Your
Heart

…

Because
10 times out of 10
It knows what's best for you.

K.

Hello Flower,

Live
Life
One day at a time.

K.

Hello Flower,

Always be truthful
...
Telling a lie
may
Be
A
Temporary fix
But it's a
Long
Term
Loss.

K.

Hello Flower,

Work
Hard
Now

...

Celebrate even harder later.

K.

Hello Flower,

Would the future you
Be happy
With all you're working towards
Today?
…
Make yourself proud.

K.

Hello Flower,

It's a beautiful thing
To
Do
For
Others
...
It's
Equally
As
Beautiful to put yourself
first
Sometimes.

K.

Hello Flower,

You
Are
Powerful
Beyond
Measure

...

Use your power to better world.

K.

Hello Flower,

Finish
What
You
Start (ed).

K.

www.ingramcontent.com/pod-product-compliance
Lightning Source LLC
Chambersburg PA
CBHW071408290426
44108CB00014B/1728